# Chapter 17

# 2003 - 2004

CW00688062

## A footnote to the history

During the early months of 2003, Pete Gripton (56B) was trying hard (some would say he's always been very trying!) to bring his compilation of the College history to a satisfactory close. Attending one of the Committee meetings to report on his progress, he was delighted to find that Ken Anderson, a 'young Jeep from 58A', was volunteering his services towards the final publication and printing. This was later to entail the pair of them in many visits to the archives of the REME Museum, where they pored diligently over the collection of photographs relating to the eight decades that covered the time-span of the School/College existence. They also found the time during each visit to repair to the local *Bramshill Hunt* for lunch – all in the name of historical research of course!

The spring/summer issue of *OBAN No.27* looked ahead towards the Annual Reunion, to be held over the weekend based on June 20th 2003. In his notes as Honorary Secretary, Lt Col (Ret'd) Bill Cleasby (61C) announced that WEN 'Bill' Pusey (46A) was finally stepping down as a Committee member, after a long and dedicated stint of some twenty-five years. On behalf of all Old Boys, he thanked Bill for all his wise counsel and wished him well for the future. The Honorary Secretary also reported on the tremendous work being put in by Ken Anderson, both in his capacity of looking after the Old Boys' Website and now in the final collation and publication of the College history, as prepared by Pete Gripton.

In the same *OBAN*, Clive Soord of 54B looked back on his three years of 'boys' service' as having had the greatest impact on his life. The basic trade training had taught him to be resourceful and, to this day, he still surprises himself – and his wife! – by the number of repair jobs he can fix with makeshift tools and bits from the 'gash box'! It must be a familiar theme in many an ex-boy's home life. Clive has attended *"a couple of reunions at Arborfield in the last ten years"* and was struck at just how much has changed in the intervening fifty years. As he says, *"nothing lasts forever and one wonders for how much longer the system of Army*

*apprentices will continue"*. He also cast doubt, in these days of political correctness, on the future of holding 'Old *Boys*' Reunions' – something that only the future will tell.

Lemmy Holmes of 54A was also in 'memory mode', having submitted a photograph of several members of his intake, taken outside Room D4 'B' Coy during 1955. They were all taking in the refined aroma and taste of Burmese cigars, sold for a few pennies by either Than Soe, Kin Nyunt, Sein Pe or Tin Nyunt – it's amazing how those names have stayed in his memory. Lemmy recalls the popularity of *'Radio Luxembourg'* in those distant days, and how makeshift aerials were cunningly erected to improve reception. Most of this seemed to consist of very long lengths of wire, draped over the barrack-room roofs. One such piece of wire, seen dangling outside the window of 'D4', was immediately plugged into the mains socket, causing a certain privately owned radio elsewhere to burst into flames!

As usual, the *OBAN* continued to serve as a great sounding board for ex-boys' tales, many of them reminiscing about days at 'the old school' and others telling of later days, spent in service across the globe. Ron Sykes was one of the original intake of 39A and recalls being bussed up to Wembley Stadium to hand out Cup Final programmes. *(Haven't heard that one before, Ron. If memory serves me correctly, didn't Portsmouth beat Wolves that year, going on to 'hold the Cup' for an unprecedented seven – albeit wartime – years? Ed.)* Going back to an older vintage, Peter Humpton, a 1938 Jersey boy, finally contacted *OBAN* from his home in Perth, West Australia, asking to be placed on the mailing list.

Sadly, the 'deceased' list tends to get a little longer in current editions, but it is great that someone has remembered and felt that the owners' names should be published as a mark of respect and fond recollection. For instance, stalwart ex-boy Paul 'Tug' Wilson of 42A finally brought the curtain down on his performance on July 31st. His widow Liz was later to add this fitting tribute to her sadly departed husband:

*"Paul has always said that the School at Arborfield was the foundation of his 'charmed life'. I am sure he was known by so many of the Old Boys, being in attendance on the OBA days every year since 1977. He was quite proud of his attendance record. I know he would want me to let all the other old boys know that that he will 'keep the bar open' for new arrivals and 'save a bedspace' on request! These were two of his favourite expressions."*

During the summer of 2003, Eddie Hind was trying to sort out his effects before a move to the Atlantic island of Tenerife. He came across some old photographs and lots of paraphernalia referring to his time at boys' school, back as a member of 52A. Two old letters stirred his memory, one from himself to his parents in Dorset and the other from his Company Commander,

*The gravestone in Arborfield Cemetery*

both of which told 'Mum and Dad' that Eddie had survived a shooting! This had occurred in barrack room 'J2', when another apprentice had accidentally let off a .22" miniature rifle that put a bullet into Eddie's right groin, and which had then *"passed through a few inches of his leg, coming out again on the inside of his thigh"*. Eddie had been rushed into the Cambridge Miltary Hospital at Aldershot and his own letter told his parents that he was fine and hoped to be out again *"within a few days"*.

The 'official letter' was more detailed and reassured Mr and Mrs Hind that their son had suffered no serious pain, apart from a certain amount of throbbing. Eddie had been x-rayed and attended by a 'surgical specialist', with the medical authorities reporting that there would be no lasting effects, once the wounds had healed. The accident occurred in 1954, so for Eddie to be sending all his letters, papers and photographs to the REME Museum for safe keeping, almost fifty years later, it is obvious that he came through his ordeal and lived to 'tell the tale'. But a mere couple of inches saved Eddie from a fate that could have threatened his lineage in no uncertain manner!

On August 20th 2003, Mrs Eveline Cook, widow of the ever-remembered Ben Cook, ex-RSM of the Army Technical School (Boys) when it first opened its gates in 1939, passed away peacefully at the grand old age of ninety-seven. Her son-in-law, John Pewsey, himself an ex-boy of the 45A intake, wrote the following:

*"I feel sure that there may still be many ex-Arborfield boys who remember Mrs Cook's kindness, by way of cups of tea and biscuits to lads like myself, who were detailed off by Ben to carry out fatigues/jankers, at one or other of his quarters up the road from the main gate".*

## Better late than never

Over the weekend of August 29th – September 1st 2003, a select gathering of Arborfield old boys, those of the 1943 intake, gathered to celebrate their 60th (Diamond) Anniversary. There were thirty-three of these self-described 'old sweats' on parade at the *Royal Court Hotel* in Coventry. The original intake of 330 boys must have been one of the largest in history, and the lack of quantity sixty years later was more than made up for by the sheer quality of those attending! Many long-

# *Supplement to The Arborfield Apprentice*
*An illustrated history of the Arborfield Army Apprentices' School and Colleges*

First Published 2004 by the Arborfield Old Boys Association
The REME Museum
Isaac Newton Road
Arborfield
RG2 9NY.

Author and Editor Peter Gripton 56B
Copyright © Arborfield Old Boys Association 2004

ISBN 0-9545142-1-1

Typeset by Ken Anderson 58A
Printed in Great Britain by The Amadeus Press Ltd., Cleckheaton, West Yorkshire.

# The Final Chapter

## A supplement to 'The Arborfield Apprentice'

Friday 13th August 2004 saw the closure of the Army Technical Foundation College, marking the end of a remarkable epoch of Army Apprentice training at Arborfield, covering a period of 65 years.

Some members of the 1943 intake together with their ladies who gathered to celebrate their 60th Anniversary

serving *(Did I also hear 'long-suffering? Ed.)* wives also graced the reunion; the expertise and elegance of the many on the dance floor was no doubt bolstered by the high calorie hotel cuisine and liquid energy. Long distance travellers included ex-boys from as far away as Taiwan and Ohio. Main organiser for the event was John Dutton (43B), still busily engaged in producing a history of REME involvement in the Korean War of the early Fifties.

*OBAN Issue 28* brought a welcome splash of colour into the lives of all who received it. The simple reason was that the front cover, plus many of the internal photographs, had been printed in colour for the first time. Proudly making an appearance on that front cover were Frank Weller (VM REME, ex-'A' Coy, Dick Wright (Draughtsman RE, ex-'C' Coy, Pete Henry (Draughtsman RE, ex-'C' Coy, Gordon Bonner (Fitter, later VM REME, ex-'D/B' Coy and Max Warwick (Armourer REME, ex-'C' Coy). They had all been members of the 1949 intakes and were attending the 2003 Reunion dinner.

The *Chairman's Message* was written by Lt Col Andy Phillips RE, the most recent (and no doubt the last) CO of the ATFC. He had attended that dinner mentioned above and expressed his delight at having been able to do so. He expressed the opinion that the AOBA was *"clearly in excellent health"*, but could not be so optimistic about the future of the ATFC itself. At the time, a 'business plan' was being put forward for the final closure of the College. He was able to announce that the 2004 Reunion would definitely still take place upon the hallowed ground of Rowcroft Barracks and looked forward to *"another outstanding occasion"*.

The report on the 2003 Reunion was left to the erudite pen of Carl Hayhurst of 53A. Despite the passing years (fifty since joining), Carl's opening thoughts, as he arrived from 'oop north' with old pal Nev Dandy, were on the delightful young female A/T who showed them to their billet. Carl reckons that he would willingly have claimed her as his granddaughter, but no doubt there was the proverbial twinkle in his eye! Carl's 'standard issue' breakfast reminded him that his heart attacks must have been brought on by his teenage diet – and promised to take up his present health-food diet again on the following Monday!

A record number of old boys attended the Reunion, with around 250 sitting down – though in rather cramped style – for dinner in the Cookhouse - or Regimental Restaurant, to give its present-day fancy title! Afterwards, the 'anniversary boys' from 1953 exercised their prerogative to be last out of the bar, having spent the evening in 'Do you remember?' mode and, as they say in northern parts, 'supping some stuff'. Carl's last thought on the occasion went as follows.

2003 Reunion Parade Inspection

*"What's the difference between a group of responsible grandfathers and a bunch of teenage boys?"* His own answer to that one was *"Not much – perhaps four pints and a couple of yarns"*.

On August 12th, 17 Platoon (Pln) enjoyed a visit to the historic boatyard down on the coast at Portsmouth. The aim of the exercise was to build up leadership qualities and to encourage some of the quieter Platoon members, so that they would find it easier to slot into their later career in the Army. The tasks throughout the day included Morse code, rock climbing, knots, minefields and handcuffs, as well as a variety of mental tests, using a computer.

A letter received at 'C' Coy, from the Road Policing Unit based at a Motorway Services near Oxford, bore testament to the quick thinking actions of several Arborfield apprentices, following a road traffic accident on the M4. One particular female apprentice was highly praised, for staying with and administering first aid to the female driver of a car that had rolled several times across the busy road. At the scene of the accident, other apprentices gave reassurance to members of the public and handed out cold drinks on what was a very hot day. In his letter, Police Constable (PC) James Dixon thanked those members of the College who had acted in a proficient and professional manner. Fortunately, the lady who had 'written off' her car suffered only minor injuries, but PC Dixon added that *"any first aid, given as soon as possible, is always a good thing"*.

Kevin 'Mitch' Mitchell of 43A wrote to *OBAN* in reference to the recently attended gathering of *"us 43'ers"* and looked forward to the forthcoming book on the Arborfield history – set to rival *'Harry Potter'* he thought! He thought it a privilege that the cover was to be *"adorned with a motley crew of 43'ers, all of whom can easily be identified by Doug Boucher"*. He also added some 'muted mutterings' in the form of the following poetic licence!

2003 Reunion - a mixed contingent of Intakes

*For AOBA, as it is now known,*
*Changes are looming, hear the groan.*
*To update a title so old in fashion*
*Will surely provoke votes of passion.*

*Once a year we assemble in part,*
*We're all determined, that I'll grant*
*Paid our subs, have a natter,*
*Lamps are swung and medals clatter.*

*News exchanged, exciting don't you think?*
*Great for a laugh whilst having a drink.*
*Certainly good for an hour or two,*
*Find out what's what and about you-know-who!*

*A good few of us remember the War,*
*Doing our bit and 'bumping' the floor!*
*Three shillings to spend, a few sweets a week,*
*Not all good times, some days were bleak.*

*Dried egg, prunes, 'pom' and Spam,*
*Food parcel from Mum, rare cake and XL jam.*
*Feeding us boys a definite strain,*
*Up for baksheesh again and again!*

*We cannot help but to reminisce,*
*Is there anything that we really miss?*
*Except for our youth, which now has gone,*
*We grin and bear it and then soldier on.*

*There's a golden thread that bonds us all,*
*As we meet again in Reunion Hall.*
*It's a mutual thing, a comprehension*
*For we who live on an Army pension.*

*Surely we should go from strength to strength,*
*For aren't we all on the same wavelength?*
*So let's carry on paying our subs*
*For the Reunion 'do' at the AOB Club.*

## The Final Countdown

In the autumn of 2003, *The Arborfield Apprentice* rose phoenix-like from the last dying embers of a long and distinguished history. Not in the form of the original School (or College) magazine, but this time as a large glossy hardback book of some 500-plus pages that covered the full history of Arborfield

Apprentices' training from 1939 until the present day. Sadly however, it also signalled the final chapter in that history, with the College's closure now inevitable.

October 16th 2003 took Bill Wenborn (ex-March 1941) to the funeral of one of his old intake, that of Peter Langley. Along with ninety-eight others, they had arrived at the famous Arborfield Gates on March 18th 1941 as part of that famous 'One Hundred Armourers'. On the 16th of the same month, another old stalwart of Arborfield finally bade us all farewell after many years of meritous service, both as a serving and retired officer (RO). Maj Ezra Rhodes died at the fine old age of ninety years. Many ex-boys will recall him as the Adjutant at what was then the Army Apprentices' School in the late Fifties. Ezra had been commissioned into the King's Own Royal Regiment (Lancaster) in June 1940 – later to become the King's Own Royal Border Regiment. His last post was as an RO in HQ REME Training Centre.

Remembrance Sunday brought 3 Platoon the honour of representing the ATFC and Regular Army at the parade held in the centre of Basingstoke. They proudly took their place besides other platoons from the Army Cadet Force, RAF Cadets, Sea Cadets, Boy Scouts and other youth organisations, as well as the Salvation Army and of course the British Legion. The apprentices were pleased to march off in second place, right behind the veterans, but found it difficult to adjust to the slow pace! A/T Steele laid a wreath on behalf of the College at the town's memorial and all later agreed that it had *proved "a moving experience"*. At the ex-Serviceman's Club later, Platoon members chatted to the veterans about their time in the Army.

Another *'Technicolor'* edition of *OBAN* was issued for winter 2003. An air of pessimism must have pervaded the ATFC, as the pending closure of apprentices' training at Arborfield loomed just over the horizon. Even the chief 'optimist by nature' Bill Cleasby had to admit that 'The Final Countdown' had now begun in earnest. After *"ten years in the job"*, *OBAN* editor Brian Hornsey decided to call it a day and his services to the Association are much appreciated. Despite the natural gloom at the College's fate, the overall impression is that the OBA will continue to thrive for many years to come.

*OBAN Issue 29* certainly gave that impression a lift, with it's usual *pot-pourri* of articles and nostalgia. Included within its pages were two separate collections of stories and memories about two members of staff who will never be forgotten by those who served as boy soldiers during their periods of tenure. First up was the first RSM of 'the School', Ben Cook, who has been a source of so many articles in previous magazines and, second, a rather less-loved character from the Fifties, in the shape of Provost Sgt Fred Silvers.

The mention of 'Fred' certainly stirred the memory bank of John Moss of 55A, who wrote in to *OBAN* from his home in Nova Scotia, alongside a photograph he had sent in, showing a happy bunch of Arborfield VMs, taken around 1957/58. John had recently got in touch with another member of his intake, Ken Farmiloe and, as it turned out, Ken displayed an amazing memory. He asked John if he was *"Moss 23234031 or Moss 23234075"*! John recalled that he was a member of the School cycling team and would often cycle down to Portsmouth and back for training. One weekend he decided he'd *"had enough of Army life"* and cycled all the way home to Leicester – only to have the proverbial flea put in his ear by his mother and be told to ride his bike straight back to Arborfield! Riding all through Sunday night, John just missed the Monday morning parade, got twenty-eight days jankers for his troubles – and also had his bike confiscated!

In December of 2003, the latest edition of '*Arborfield Informer*', the ATFC Newsletter, contained an article by A/T Tootle, entitled '*Friendship and Teamwork*'. Despite the brevity of today's introductory course at Arborfield, the sentiments expressed by young Tootle show that, for budding apprentices entering the Army for the first time, what is on offer is very much in the vein of what it has always been. Namely, the chance to engage with other youngsters, be they Brummies, Scousers or Geordies etc and, by working together in the right spirit of comradeship, be prepared to enter adult life with a strong mission. The article's title seems to say it all.

### A/T Tootle's Article:

*"The article that I have chosen to write is different, as I have not focused on a particular event or landmark. The reason I have done this is that, where people have written about exercise or drill tests, they have just written about the event and not how it was accomplished, by teamwork and bonds of friendship. I have chosen to write about this, because I believe it is the root of our success.*

*The friendships that I have made over the last few weeks have been out of this world. I think this is amazing, considering the various places we come from, all over the United Kingdom. We only seem to ever disagree about which music is going to be played. Personally, my friendships started when I arrived late in my section, where they were having a meeting with the section commander, Cpl Swords. He showed me where I would be staying and my room. When I got there, all the other lads were already there, which made me very nervous of the new environment, as well as the lads themselves. I thought I would not get on with any of them but, to my surprise, we all got on very well and are now best mates.*

*The only problem with us all is our accents, as we can never understand what anyone else is saying. This can cause problems, especially when a 'Brummie' is trying to understand a 'Scouser'. There have been countless times when we have accomplished very difficult tasks and duties by working at them together. There have also been difficult times, when people have wanted to go home, but have stayed because of the comradeship. We have worked as a team on our exercises, where everyone has 'chipped in' and helped each other, on digging shell scrapes and other tasks, which would never have happened in 'civvy street'.*

*The night before our drill test, we were up until the early hours, making sure that the block was immaculate for inspection. No-one went to bed until everything was done, which paid off the next day at the inspection by Maj Norman and CSM Coates. This went extremely well and we passed with flying colours. Our drill test also went well, as everyone put in 100 per cent and worked hard as a Platoon. As a reward, we got to go to Reading and stock up on McDonalds, which, after six weeks, was superb! It was also one of the proudest moments of my life. When I told my Mum, she burst into tears, as she knew how nervous I had been about passing and she was very happy for me.*

*I hope this article has explained a small part about what it is like to be a recruit in the British Army. Although you have your bad times, you have more than enough good ones, due to the friendship and teamwork, which will last a lifetime."*

At the beginning of the New Year, the British Services X Boys' Association (BSXBA) issued its Newsletter No.33, proving that it is still a thriving entity out in New Zealand. BSXBA consists of a three-service membership, including a number of ex-boys from Arborfield. Their 2003 reunion had recently been held in Auckland and a number of them had attended the Armistice Parade, where the REME Standard was again proudly flown. The Association's 2004 reunion is being planned to take place in the Hawke's Bay area, probably based on Napier. AOBA wishes them well in their endeavours.

On Saturday 21st February, a group of twenty-two College members set off for a week's adventurous training, which was to consist of skiing in the Alps at Serre Chevalier. First impressions were naturally mixed, and A/T Shaw of 6 Pln found that he had never fallen flat on his face so many times! But skills and confidence grew as the week went on and serious injuries were happily avoided. Techniques in turning were honed, with body position and all-round control being steadily improved. At the end of the week, young Shaw was able to report that *"the whole skiing expedition is one that I shall never forget. I have never been so scared or had so much fun. Given the chance, I would do it all again"*.

## Closure Announced

In the March 2004 edition of *The Craftsman*, under the heading *'Closure Announced'*, came the following ministerial statement from the Parliamentary Under Secretary of State for Defence:

*"In my statement to the House on 27 November 2003, I announced that I had approved in principle, and subject to full Trades Union consultation, plans by the Army Training and Recruiting Agency (ATRA) to close the Army Technical Foundation College (ATFC) at Arborfield and transfer students to, principally, the Army Foundation College (AFC) at Harrogate, where a technical training stream will be introduced.*

*There will be other changes to the way in which junior recruits are trained within the ATRA, but these do not envisage closures of any establishments. I can now conform that the consultation exercise has been concluded and no serious objections have been raised to the proposal. I have therefore agreed that the closure plans may be implemented.*

*Training at the College will therefore cease with effect from August of this year (the last students being accepted at the beginning of this month (January 2004) and the College will close in March 2005. The principal aim of this proposal is to improve the*

*quality and efficiency of training provided to junior entrants to the technical trades. It will not affect the Army's commitment or ability to accept suitable junior applicants at either the AFC or other ATRA Junior Entry establishments. I do not anticipate that this will have any major impact on the Army's recruiting plans in general".*

Coincidentally, an article on the same page of that magazine was submitted by Col Nigel Moore MBE, a former CO at the College (1996-98). His article was headed up as *'Embrace change before it grabs you by the throat!'* No doubt there are thousands of ex-apprentices out there who would say that there was one 'change' that they had hoped never to embrace, but now that it had 'grabbed them by the throat', there was little more that they could do about it!

The 'beginning of the end', as one famous man may have phrased it, was of course wrapped up in 'officialese' under the banner of 'modernisation and rationalisation'. The ATRA announced that it was *"restructuring and improving the way in which Junior Entry (JE) training is currently provided"*, adding that *"the current ATFC course is neither challenging ... ... ... nor long enough"*. (*Hard to argue with that, but how did we get to that position? Ed.*) The other news, as covered in a later edition of *The Craftsman*, was that *"under the Defence Training Review ... ... ... the whole Arborfield site is a candidate to be alienated, as the Defence individual training community consolidates onto fewer, larger sites"*. The article went on to add that, *"as a lodger unit, it would be uneconomical to operate ATFC in isolation at Arborfield"*.

On March 8th 2004, members of the ATFC woke up to *'No Smoking Day'*, during which, instead of the usual hot air, the College was filled with fresh air! In order to assist in the 'ciggie-free' day, three teams arrived from the Tri-Service Dental Agency Hygiene School in Aldershot. They diligently went about their 'conversion' work, while a poster design competition was held, in order to promote the day's event. This was subsequently won by A/T Driver from 2 Pln, who won £50 worth of music vouchers. (*I can't imagine just how many '45s' that would have bought in my day! Ed.*)

Just a few days later, the last ever Army Foundation College Cup soccer match took place at Arborfield, between the home side and their opponents from Harrogate. With the benefits of a home ground and spurred on by a vociferous crowd, ATFC Arborfield soon took control of the game and ran up an unassailable 3 – 0 lead by half-time. Even though they *"took their foot off the pedal"* in the second half, making some substitutions, the final 4 – 0 win fairly reflected the *"crisp passing and fitness"* of the Arborfield side. On that same Sunday, March 14th, a similar result was achieved by the rugby team, who ran up a score of 28 to 7 against the same opponents, with four members of the side later being selected to play for the Army under-19 team.

Ray Doughty of 61B recently viewed the AAS video and enjoyed the story of the car in the static water tank, as told by old colleague 'Bugs' Hutchins. To put the record straight, Ray contacted the AOBA Website and said that, early in 1964, Austin Frith had decided he had to rid himself of the car, so one quiet evening a number of 9 Div 61B intake gently eased the car into the static water tank. 61B then passed out from the AAS in April 64, with a number of them proceeding to the SEE for a six-month 2nd Class Radar Tech course. One fine morning, Austin was summoned and departed the class at top speed. Unfortunately for him, the car had been found and traced back to him! The result – Austin returned to the course without his stripe. Ray goes on to recall his *"two years in a holiday camp spider called the Army Apprentice School"*, under the parental eye of CSM Roberts, Scots Guards – commonly known as 'The Beast'.

In late March 2004, Pete Gripton was surprised to hear the 'Gidday' Aussie accent on the phone after his wife had said. *"There's a guy called Robin Moore wants to speak to you"*. The guy in question was – and still is – an ex-boy from 58A, who was in England following his brother's sad death. Robin, or Bob, as he was probably better known to his intake, had ordered the Arborfield history book to be delivered to an address in England, saving the prohibitive postage to Sydney, where he now lives. Back to the phone call! Bob (shall we now call him that?) was calling from Northolt and wanted Pete to sign his book! The outcome was that Bob visited Pete and, over a couple of hours and a mug of coffee, had a great time reminiscing over old times and names and faces familiar to both. Pete's phone number had been passed on to Bob by mutual old pal Paul Hudson, another ex-58A old boy – so 'the network' still works well!

## A watershed for REME training

The May edition of *The Craftsman* magazine brought further proof of the downsizing in the Army and the unrelenting focus on cost cutting in the training budget. It was announced that April 1st 2004 had *"marked a watershed in REME training, when the REME Training Group (RTG) was disestablished, and its three Schools were re-organised under the federated Defence Colleges of Electro-Mechanical and Aeronautical Engineering"*. The article went on to describe the fact that a coordinated REME training organisation had been in existence since the formation of the Corps, and quoted the following from *'Craftsmen of the Army, Volume 1'*:

*"In 1942, it was decided to increase the size and scope of the Arborfield School. The new establishment included a Brigadier as Commandant, and courses were now included for officers on organisation, for soldiers in weapon training, and for boys and women of the ATS on technical instruction."*

Gordon Bonner presenting the Bell to Lt Col McAvoy

It is to be hoped that present-day readers of the REME magazine were not scratching their heads over the term *"boys and women of the ATS"*. Ex-Arborfield boys of the era will long remember the confusion and embarrassment that was caused by the 'ATS' title that rightly described both the boys of the Army Technical School and the ladies of the Auxiliary Territorial Service! It was to be as late as 1947 that the School eventually became the Army Apprentices' School.

*OBAN Issue 30* was brought out in the spring of 2004, carrying with it the invitations for attendance at the 2004 Reunion, definitely the last one to be held on the site of the original Army Technical School (Boys). On current planning, Rowcroft Barracks is due to finally close down in April of 2005. Bill Cleasby looked forward to the completion of a facsimile of Poperinghe Guardroom being ready to greet visitors to the REME Museum at the Reunion weekend. *(Is there any truth in the rumour that the Guardroom is being held open in readiness for any ex-boys who misbehave at the Reunion? Ed.)*

An article in the same magazine came from Gordon Bonner (49B). Prior to his retirement, whilst serving at 26 Command Wksp in Scotland, he had come across an old bell, which dated back to around 1898, now sadly discarded and thrown into a skip. Gordon had taken the old bell home, where it was then used as a doorstop for the next twelve years. But, having found out about the Guardroom project (as mentioned above), he was happy to refurbish and donate the bell as a genuine piece of military equipment to what seemed like a natural home.

Johnny Johnson of 56B provided a follow-up story to that one told in *Issue 26*, recounting his three-year sentence here at Arborfield. He now continued by telling of his escapades upon moving into the wide new world of REME service with the Regular Army, in much the same vein as the many other stories that have graced the pages of the *OBAN* since its re-introduction in early 1992. Ken Anderson reported on his recent move to Peniscola, located halfway between Barcelona and Valencia in Spain, from where he would continue to manage the AOBA Website. On his way to Spain, he had called in on David Schofield (65A), the previous Webmaster, at his home in the French town of Limoges. *(They do get about, these Webmasters, don't they! Does it go with the job? How does one qualify? Ed.)* The usual high standard of magazine articles prevailed, with contributions from far and wide.

On Monday May 10th, the Old Boys' Management Committee met for what was likely to be the penultimate time in its time-honoured format. With the impending demise of the ATFC, the military members of that Committee, in the shape of the CO, his Adjutant and the RSM, would no longer be around to add their expertise to the matters in hand. On behalf of all ex-boys, Hon Sec Bill Cleasby offered a heartfelt thank-you to the present incumbents, as well as all their predecessors, for all the unstinting hard work that had been put in over a great number of years.

The Committee looked forward to the forthcoming Reunion with a certain amount of trepidation! Due to the fact that this was to be the last one held here at Rowcroft, applications for attendance had already reached record-breaking proportions. Some wag did add that perhaps there were many coming along just to make sure that the place was definitely closing! Whatever the case, John Smithson came along to the meeting to propose that a full video recording be made

WO1 Osborne PWRR - the last RSM

Marching in to Rowcroft Barracks for the Final Reunion

of the great occasion and the Committee gave the plan its blessing, provided that the details could be agreed in the interim period. Many will recall the video produced by John at the 1997 Reunion.

A survey held on the AOBA Website indicated great support for the continuation of the Association, with the majority hoping that future Reunions would still be held in Arborfield for the foreseeable future. The Honorary Secretary explained that these would perhaps be held more as 'open days' at Hazebrouck Barracks. No doubt there would be lively discussion at the 2004 AGM.

**Final Reunion at Rowcroft**

They began arriving on Friday June 18th and it seemed like an invasion by the Mongol hordes! It was a joy to see so many old boys turning up to celebrate sixty-five years of Arborfield history, though tinged with the sad realisation that this would be the final Reunion to be held on the site of the original ATS (Boys). Many of those arriving were doing so for the very first time and it was obvious from the looks upon their faces that they wished they had decided to 'do it' much earlier.

Sales of the College history, *'The Arborfield Apprentice'*, were brisk, with the general opinion that it had been a job well worth doing, and timed to perfection with the closure of the College now just around the corner. Thanks once again to the College RSM, WO1 Neil Osborne, Princess of Wales's Royal Regiment (PWRR), the Sgts' Mess provided the venue for the evening, as literally hundreds of ex-boys gathered together to swap yarns and 'swing the lamp'. *(With beer and lager at a pound a pint, there seemed to be an awful lot of liquid refreshment to oil the parched throats too! Ed)*

The Reunion followed the well established pattern of previous years, with the Drum Head service and proud march-past made memorable by the fine sunshine and record numbers of those 'on parade'. For the first time, the parade was split into Platoons, each one representing an era from the College – and School – history. Naturally enough, it was the 'thirty-niners' and their ilk who led off, with not a little pomp and swagger in their stride. *(There is no truth in the remark that they were only at the front because, if they'd been at the rear they'd never have kept up! Only joking! Ed.)* In the event, it was as good a performance on that old Square as had ever graced it previously.

Highly noticeable during the day's events was the presence of the film crew, present to 'videotape' the whole event as a living memento of the success of the College itself and its ex-apprentices in particular. At the evening's AGM, it was unanimously agreed that every effort be made to continue holding the reunion at Arborfield for as long as there are facilities available. Following the meeting, dinner was served in the College Restaurant, where the apprentices of today successfully performed the almost impossible task of keeping some 360 hungry ex-apprentices well served with their hot food – and there were no cries of 'Plates' to upset the discerning diner! As well as the after-dinner speech from the Chairman, Lt Col Andy Phillips, it was left to Howard Trill (54A) to present a representative address on behalf of those boys from the two 1954 intakes, on the occasion of their 50th Anniversary.

Howard trawled through his memory bank to recall some of the incidents that had made their time at Arborfield so memorable. On the day that the firework factory put on its most spectacular display, two apprentices on Fire Picket duty made the grisly find of a boot with a foot still inside it. A couple of PTIs rescued barrels of gunpowder from the factory, rolling them down Biggs Lane with their feet, whilst balanced upon them like lumberjacks. Howard added that, *"the Reunion had its sadder side, as we accepted the inevitability of a last look at where our military life had begun"*. He likened the occasion to that of being in a Time Machine, where the inhabitants had grown *"crinkled and wrinkled – but no change in the characters we knew so many years ago"*.

'Mitch' Mitchell of 43A, a regular poetic

Standard flying - we marched past as proudly as we did all those years ago!

contributor to the pages of the newsletter, later sent in this verse, which aptly sums up the day's activities and festivities in his usual inimitable style!

**The Grand Finale**

*Last parade on hallowed ground we're told,*
*Its demise looms close, it's all to be sold.*
*Last parade on our dear old Square –*
*So many memories linger there.*

*"From the right – number! Make it snappy!"*
*"Shout louder please, I'm a deaf grandpappy!"*
*We're sorted out with much precision*
*In Platoons formed up – or was it Divisions?*

*"A good turnout lads", or so they said.*
*Or were they polite cos we're grey in the head?*
*Smartly we marched, all as good as each other,*

AOB Association Honorary Secretary Bill Cleasby and friend Maurice Britton in the early 1960s.

*Proudly pleased that we all took the bother.*

*How memories surged, marching through that gate,*
*Spurred on by the REME Band – just great.*
*On the Square, medals gleamed like treasure,*
*Just like yesteryear and what a pleasure.*

*Come the last PoP of College fame,*
*Dare they let some Old Boys share the same?*
*Whatever happenings the future may hold,*
*The memories will stay, no matter what's sold!*

During the evening's celebrations, an almost ancient newspaper cutting came to light. *(Unfortunately it was not dated and I cannot recall who provided it! However, stories in 'The Arborfield Apprentice' Chapter 5 would place the event in the very early Fifties. Ed.).* It referred to the unsavoury incident of many years ago, when Provost Sgt Fred Silvers had suffered the indignity of being stabbed by one of his own Provost staff. No reference is made to the reason behind the attack, other than the story that twenty-four year old L/Cpl Francis Joseph Kelly had drunk *"fifteen pints of beer in Wokingham on the night of the incident".* At Berkshire Assizes in Reading, the presiding judge, Mr Justice Cassells, announced, *"I think the court is entitled to investigate this matter to the full. If this is the type of conduct that goes on in that unit, it is high time some clearance was made. And if the Wokingham public-houses can pour fifteen pints of beer down the throat of one young man in one night, it is high time some drastic action was taken against them".* Whether or not this statement was followed by any action is not reported.

Local newspaper, the *Reading Evening Post,* reported on *"an invasion of nearly 400 former soldiers, when old boys from their soon-to-be-axed Army College enjoyed what may be their last get-together there".* The report continued: *"The Army Technical Foundation College, formerly known as the Army Technical School, opened on May 1st 1939, four months before the start of the Second World War. But new Government proposals mean (that) Arborfield Garrison, which also houses soldiers from the Royal Electrical and Mechanical Engineers (REME) and the School of Electronic and Aeronautical Engineering (SEAE), is likely to close by 2008. The Army College is the first casualty, when it stops taking recruits in*

*August this year and closes fully next year."*

## The last Passing-out Parade ('Pop')

On Monday 12th July, Rowcroft Sergeants' Mess saw the final meeting of the AOBA Management Committee in its time-honoured format. Lt Col Andy Phillips (CO), Capt Eric Warren (Adjutant) and RSM Osborne have carried on in the glorious tradition of their many illustrious successors, in 'aiding and abetting' the Old Boys' Association in keeping alive the *esprit de corps*, so movingly developed over the previous sixty-five years. It was agreed that video footage of the forthcoming 'Final PoP', to take place in August 2004, will be added to that recorded during the last Reunion at Rowcroft. This should make a memorable record of the final days here at Arborfield.

And so, on Thursday 12th August, they came in their thousands – literally – to attend the final 'PoP' at the Army Technical Foundation College. Friends, sweethearts, parents, brothers, sisters and whole families of all ages poured through the College gates.

The rain did its utmost to dampen spirits during the early part of the day, but nothing could take away the undoubted good will that was flowing through the gathered throng. Dodging the showers, which were often accompanied by intervals of almost scorching sunshine, was the order of the morning. Within the female congregation, summer dresses were in abundance, as well as the proverbial 'shirt-sleeve order' worn by their menfolk. Umbrellas came in handy too at times! But there was also a contingent of more elderly gentlemen in view, mostly dressed in their best suits, with not a few of them proudly sporting their collections of medals.

These were some of the Arborfield 'Old Boys', who had come back to their old stamping ground to honour the latest – and last – generation of apprentices to pass out of their famous College – or School, as it had been in their day. Indeed, there were amongst their ranks several members of the original 1939A intake, who had 'came, seen and marched' on the very first 'PoP'. No doubt to them it felt like a rather sad occasion, but definitely also a very proud one. The College has been

After just eight months of training, Intake 04A is as smart as any other intake has been.

lovingly known as 'the boys' school' for most of its sixty-five years, this despite the fact that for the last ten years (since 1994) girls have also been allowed to study as apprentices.

The programme of events for the final 'PoP' is shown below:

---

1000 hrs Guests seated (areas for AOBA/ATFC PS)

1005 hrs VIPs seated

1005 hrs Markers

1010 hrs Parade marches on

1017 hrs Officers' Call

1013 hrs The Reviewing Officer arrives

1030-1145 hrs The Parade
    General Salute
    Inspection
    March past in quick time
    Advance in Review Order
    General Salute
    Presentation of Passing-out Awards and Medals
    Address by Reviewing Officer
    Prayers and Blessing
    Divisions march off
    Band marches off

1145-1200 hrs Royal Signals White Helmets Display

1200-1210 hrs Final march-off led by CO
          (Old Boys/PS past and present)

1210 hrs Reviewing Party departs to display area

1245 hrs Reviewing Party meets prize winners

1315 hrs Reviewing Party departs to Mess

1315-1500 hrs Officers' Mess luncheon

1500 hrs Guests and Intake 04A disperse

---

The crowds milled around within the College complex. There were display tents provided by the four elements of the training system – the REME, RE, R Sigs and RLC – while the Regimental Restaurant provided refreshments and a place to shelter from the showers. The question on everyone's lips must have

concerned that rain and its effect upon the forthcoming parade. Thankfully the weather gods looked down kindly and, from the moment the parade started at 10.00 hrs, only a few drops of drizzle managed to disturb the gathered spectators as the grand spectacle got under way.

What a stirring sight as the apprentices of 04A marched onto the Square. Not the original 'old Square', now sadly relegated to providing the car park, but nevertheless uplifting the spirits and musically enhanced by the presence of the Band of the Royal Irish Regiment, ably assisted by the Pipes and Corps of Drums provided by the College itself. The parade was reviewed by the Adjutant General, Lt Gen Sir Alastair Irwin KCB, CBE, who afterwards addressed the parade and presented the prizes.

As the apprentices marched off to the strains of *Auld Lang Syne*, there must have been many a damp eye and lumps in many a throat. But these were soon chased away by the thrilling performance of the Royal Signals *'White Helmets'* Motorcycle Display Team, who entertained the crowd for around half-an-hour. Then finally, the last march-past, as a contingent of College old boys and members of the Permanent Staff bade their own fond farewell. Never have sinews been so strained – shoulders back, tummies held in and arms swinging – as the grand occasion was brought to such a nostalgic finish. After some sixty-five years of apprentices' training at Arborfield, the last 'Pop' had taken place.

During the day, video cameras whirred, capturing the spirit of the occasion. This has become the custom in recent years, with parents and families able to purchase a copy of their sons' and/or daughters' passing-out parade. On this particular day, some of the footage that was taken, particularly that of the Old Boys proud march-past, will be added on to the video (and DVD?) that was recorded at the last Reunion.

A splendid souvenir brochure/programme was produced for that final parade and will no doubt be treasured in years to come by those who managed to get their hands on a copy. The 'Foreword' in that brochure was written by the Rt Hon Viscount Alanbrooke of Brookeborough, former College lecturer Victor Brooke. His words are reproduced below:

*"Congratulations to those who are passing out today and a very big welcome to all the parents, guardians and friends who have come to*

witness this very proud day. I would also like to thank the military and civilian staff who, in the last twenty-eight weeks, have ensured that these young people achieved their aim.

This parade is the proud conclusion of their Apprentice Foundation Course. Sadly, though, it is also the end of a remarkable epoch. The training of boy soldiers stretches back in history, but the training of young tradesmen goes back to just after the First World War, when recruits with engineering training were needed to meet the demands of an increasingly mechanised Army. Boys volunteered to join at fifteen-and-a-half years old and they were given a three-year course of all-round education, in addition to technical and military training.

The first major Apprentices' School was established at Chepstow in 1923. The aim of the Army Apprentice system since then has changed little. It has been an outstanding success, with many thousands of Apprentices passing through the gates, not only here at Arborfield, but also Chepstow, Carlisle and Harrogate, as well as several smaller schools such as Jersey and Hilsea, which have become but faint memories.

The young men and women you see before you are, in many ways, little different from those who preceded them – turning up with hope and nervous enthusiasm and leaving with confidence and pride. To them I wish good fortune, happiness and success in their new career. Perhaps they will remember too that they are the continuation of a great tradition of Army Apprentices.

RSM Osborne stands proudly to attention for the final parade

*Perhaps, as others before them, they will achieve high rank, like Maj Gen John Stokoe CB CBE, an ex-apprentice from Harrogate, and former Arborfield Apprentices Col Mike Dorward MBE, Col Barry Keast and Lt Col (soon to be Col) Derek McAvoy, who all later in their lives returned to command the College.*

*We should not forget, however, the multitude of former members of staff, both military and civilian, some of whom are here today. With their experience, tradition and not a little patience, they helped to train, shape and look after generations of apprentice tradesmen. To them, the Army and the country owe a considerable debt."*

Victor went on to thank the CO for inviting him to write the foreword for the final 'PoP'. Having himself served at both Chepstow and Arborfield, he counted himself most fortunate to have been part of the proud past of the Army Apprentices' story.

*OBAN 31* made its appearance towards the end of the year, with a message from the new, though very familiar, Chairman, Col (Ret'd) Peter Gibson. Col Peter had assumed the post after the final Passing-out Parade and only then realised the significance and coincidence behind that date of August 10th. It was exactly ten years to the day that he had ceased to be the Commandant of what was then the Princess Marina College. Association members will be aware that in the intervening years, Peter has been very instrumental in keeping alive the spirit of the Old Boys' Association and recruiting many new - and old - faces to the ranks. It was fitting that final messages of 'farewell and good luck' came from outgoing Chairman, Lt Col Andy Phillips, and his staunch supporters, Adjutant Capt Eric Warren and WO1 (RSM) Neil Osborne.

Contributions to the *OBAN* continued to be many and varied. Howard Trill of 54A followed up his after-dinner Reunion speech with a report on his thoughts of being *"fifty years on"*, while Dave Perrott of 49B sent in the words of a song that summed up the whole Reunion weekend. Memories of long ago, from ex-boys of many generations, whetted the appetite and hopefully provided the spur for many other such stories to appear in future issues. For it is only by the constant exchange of stories and nostalgia that the magazine will continue to flourish. The site of our youthful adventures may have now closed, but the spirit will hopefully live on for many years to come.

The mixed contingent of Permanent Staff and Old Boys at the Final 'PoP' on August 12, 2004.

## The College Badge

In the programme issued to commemorate the last Passing-out Parade, a poem was reproduced, thought to have *"first appeared in a magazine in 1955"* and which *"explains the meaning (of the badge) admirably"*. That poem is again produced below, although the author is *"Anon"*.

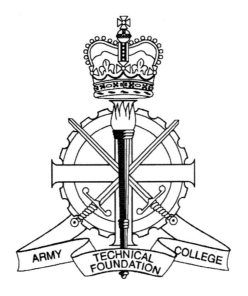

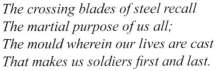

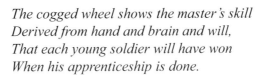

*The crossing blades of steel recall*
*The martial purpose of us all;*
*The mould wherein our lives are cast*
*That makes us soldiers first and last.*

*The cogged wheel shows the master's skill*
*Derived from hand and brain and will,*
*That each young soldier will have won*
*When his apprenticeship is done.*

*The burning torch denotes the course*
*Of learning, which began at source;*
*We follow since we know the need*
*Of learning in those meant to lead.*

*These emblems three support above*
*The Royal Emblem of our love;*
*St Edward's Crown in all its sheen,*
*Proud sign of all who serve the Queen.*

*Embracing all there is the Cross,*
*Without which all is surely loss;*
*That those who wear the badge may feel*
*Their duty is a great deal.*

# Annex to Chapter 17

## Lt Col A W 'Andy' Phillips RE

Lt Col Phillips was commissioned into the Royal Engineers in 1985, having obtained a degree in politics from Swansea University. After completing the RE Young Officer course, he served as a Troop Commander in 39

Engineer Regt and then as an Assistant Instructor in the Field Engineer Wing at the RSME in Chatham, Kent. A tour as the Adjutant of 25 Eng Regt in Osnabruck was followed by two years as the British Exchange Officer at the Canadian School of Military Engineering in Chilliwack, British Columbia.

In 1995, he served on the staff of 24 Airmobile Bde in Colchester, a tour which included an operational deployment to the former Republic of Yugoslavia. In 1996 he moved to HQ RSME at Minley, where he was responsible for setting up the Competing for Quality (CFQ) project. Having gained his Masters Degree in Defence Technology from the RMCS at Shrivenham, he attended his first Joint Command and Staff Course at Bracknell.

In 1998, Andy took command of 21 Fld Sqn (Explosive Ordnance disposal) and had the privilege of commanding the Squadron on operations in Kosovo. Between 2000 and 2003, he was employed as a staff officer in the MoD, firstly as an SO2 in

The last Commanding Officer Lt Col Andy Philips RE

the Directorate of Equipment Capability (Direct Battlefield Engagement) and then as an S01 in the Directorate of Equipment Planning. The latter post included responsibility for the co-ordination of all Urgent Operational Requirements for operations in Iraq.

He took command of the ATFC on June 20th 2003 and, following the closure of the College on the 13th August 2004, he assumed command of 1 RSME at Chatham. Andy is married to Fiona and has two sons, Robert and James. He is a keen sportsman, having represented the RE at both football and cricket. At the time of writing he was currently the Chairman of the RE Cricket Club.

# Post Scriptum

*'It ain't over till the fat lady sings'* goes a phrase in common use today. Well, I'm afraid the fat lady has well and truly sung now and, as far as 'the boys' school' is concerned, it is definitely 'over'. My compilation of the history of apprentices' training at Arborfield ended at a point where closure seemed inevitable, but was still not officially sanctioned. That point was reached during the summer months of 2003 and this *'post scriptum'* – which means 'written afterwards' – fills in the gap that would have existed between then and the final cessation of training in August 2004.

I was fortunate enough to attend the final Passing-out Parade held at the ATFC and that was followed by very mixed feelings, a certain amount of sadness but also a tremendous sense of pride. As I drove home across the border between Berkshire and Hampshire, a warm glow was engendered – and it wasn't due to the car heater alone! The College may have closed, but the spirit and comradeship of its Old Boys will continue for many a long year. I hope that this 'final chapter' sets the seal upon the traditions and *esprit de corps* so carefully nurtured over the last sixty-five years.

*Peter Gripton, October 2004.*

# Commandants at Arborfield

The first Commandant and Chief Instructor was Col F A Hilborn, MBE (late RAOC) who apart from a break of twelve months (November 1939 – November 1940), during which time Col P G Davies, CMG, CBE was in post, held the chair from the opening May 1st 1939, the opening day, until September 1943.

## Commandants

| | | | |
|---|---|---|---|
| 1 | May 1939/Nov 1939 | Col F A Hilborn | late RAOC |
| 2 | Nov 1939/Nov 1940 | Col P G Davies | |
| 1 | Nov 1940/Sep 1943 | Col F A Hilborn | |
| 3 | 1943/47 | Col J D White | late RAOC |
| 4 | 1947/49 | Col Grenville-Grey | late KRRC |
| 5 | 1949/52 | Col E L Percival | late HLI |
| 6 | 1952/55 | Col F A H Magee | late East Surreys |
| 7 | 1955/58 | Col J R Cole | late The Loyals |
| 8 | 1958/62 | Col R F D Legh | late Royal Artillery |
| 9 | 1962/65 | Col J L Dobie | REME |
| 10 | 1965/68 | Col G W Paris | REME |
| 11 | 1968/70 | Col D A Brown | REME |
| 12 | 1970/73 | Col E G Bailey | REME |
| 13 | 1973/76 | Col H K Tweed | REME |
| 14 | 1976/79 | Col B G Keast | REME |
| 15 | 1979/83 | Col J D C Peacock | REME |
| 16 | 1983/85 | Col S J Roberts | REME |
| 17 | 1985/88 | Col A A Soar | REME |
| 18 | 1988/91 | Col P H Kay | REME |
| 19 | 1991/94 | Col P H Gibson | REME |
| 20 | 1994/95 | Col M C Dorward | REME |
| 21 | 1995/96 | Lt Col R Mount | REME |

## Commanding Officers

| | | | |
|---|---|---|---|
| 22 | 1996/98 | Lt Col N Moore | REME |
| 23 | 1998/00 | Lt Col J W Mitchell | RE |
| 24 | 2000/03 | Lt Col D A McAvoy | REME |
| 25 | 2003/04 | Lt Col A Philips | RE |

# Regimental Sergeant Majors

## Army Technical School (Boys)

| | | | |
|---|---|---|---|
| 1 | 1939-Apr 41 | WO1 RSM H E Cook | Grenadier Guards |
| 2 | May 41-Feb 47 | WO1 RSM R L McNally | Scots Guards |

## Army Apprentices School

| | | | |
|---|---|---|---|
| 2 | Feb 47-Sep 56 | WO1 RSM R L McNally | Scots Guards |
| 3 | Sep 56-Jun 60 | WO1 RCM J T Sallis | Royal Horse Guards |
| 4 | Jun 60-Jan 63 | WO1 RSM J Stewart | Irish Guards |
| 5 | Jan 63-Apr 66 | WO1 RSM H Simpson | Coldstream Guards |
| 6 | Apr 66-Oct 66 | WO1 RSM D McMahon | Grenadier Guards |

## Army Apprentices College

| | | | |
|---|---|---|---|
| 6 | Oct 66-Apr 69 | WO1 RSM D M McMahon | Grenadier Guards |
| 7 | Apr 69-Jan 71 | WO1 RSM R G Woodfield | Grenadier Guards |
| 8 | Jan 71-Sep 72 | WO1 RSM D Delgarno | Scots Guards |
| 9 | Sep 72-Jul 74 | WO1 RSM C Petherick | Coldstream Guards |
| 10 | Jul 74-May 78 | WO1 RSM H V Meredith | Irish Guards |
| 11 | May 78-Oct 79 | WO1 RSM L Perkins | Grenadier Guards |
| 12 | Oct 79-Jan 80 | WO1 RSM D Cummings | Grenadier Guards |
| 13 | Jan 80-May 81 | WO1 RSM D P Yorke | Coldstream Guards |

## Princess Marina College

| | | | |
|---|---|---|---|
| 13 | May 81-Dec 81 | WO1 RSM D P Yorke | Coldstream Guards |
| 14 | Dec 81-Aug 83 | WO1 RSM A Fox | Coldstream Guards |
| 15 | Aug 83-May 86 | WO1 RSM J H Todd | Coldstream Guards |
| 16 | May 86-Jul 88 | WO1 RSM A Milloy | Scots Guards |
| 17 | Aug 88-Jun 90 | WO1 RSM N F Hartley | Coldstream Guards |
| 18 | Jul 90-Apr 92 | WO1 RSM M Burns | Irish Guards |
| 19 | Apr 92-Dec 93 | WO1 RSM D Murray | Scots Guards |
| 20 | Dec 93-Sep 95 | WO1 RSM J F Rowell | Grenadier Guards |
| 21 | Sep 95-Aug 97 | WO1 RSM R L P Matthews | REME |
| 22 | Aug 97-Oct 99 | WO1 RSM P B Rooney | Welsh Guards |
| 23 | Oct 99-Sep 00 | WO1 RSM W T Emmerson | Coldstream Guards |

## Army Technical Foundation College

| | | | |
|---|---|---|---|
| 23 | Sep 00-Nov 01 | WO1 RSM W T Emmerson | Coldstream Guards |
| 24 | Jan 02-July 03 | WO1 RSM D G Mullens | Coldstream Guards |
| 25 | July 03 - Aug 04 | WO1 RSM N T Osborne | PWRR |

# Index

# Notes

# ARMY APPRENTICES SCHOOL
## ARBORFIELD

# Passing-out Ceremony
### 25th July, 1952

Inspecting Officer:

**GENERAL SIR OUVRY L. ROBERTS,**
K.C.B., K.B.E., D.S.O., A.D.C.
General Officer Commanding-in-Chief Southern Command

Apprentices Commanding the Parade:

A.C.S.M. WILLIAMS, P. J. "C" Coy.

---

This Senior Division now passing out arrived at Arborfield in September, 1949, and will shortly be posted, as Class III Tradesmen, to units throughout the Regular Army.

During its three years at the School, the Division has been well represented in the School sports teams, and the following members of the Division have been awarded School Colours:

**Cross Country.** Coy.
A/T Castells, J. - - "C"

**Boxing.**
A.C.S.M. Williams, P.J. -
A/Cpl. Pearson, D. - - "C"
A/Sgt. Thornton, J. - - "A"

**Hockey.**
A/Cpl. Bowden, E. - - "B"
A/L/Cpl. Vaughan, J. - "A"

**Soccer.** Coy.
A/Cpl. M. Chaffey, J. G. (Capt.) "B"
A/Sgt. Mather, G. L. - "A"
A/Sgt. Charlwood, L. - "C"
A/T. Revells, D. L. - "C"

**Athletics.**
A/Sgt. Wright, R. (Capt.) "C"
A/L/Cpl. Rogers, N. - "C"
A/T. Fawcett, C. W. - "B"

**Cricket.**
A/T. Baker, R. (Capt.) "C"
A/L/Cpl. Chance, D. S. "A"
A/T. Rennie, D. L. - "C"

**.22in. Miniature Rifle Shooting.**
A/T. Jordan, P. A. (Capt.) "A"

* Indicates a "double" Colour.

A badge for P.T. was awarded to A/Cpl. Sylvester, B. "C" Coy.

The remaining Divisions at the School (together with the Senior) are divided into Companies, denoted by different coloured lanyards on the shoulder straps of their jackets: "A" Company—maroon; "B" Company—red; "C" Company—green; and "H.Q." Company, consisting of the Junior Division, wears no colour.

The honour of carrying the Champion Companies' Banner, and being termed as the Champion Company throughout the year, goes to the Company which has come out top in the annual revolving for a Competition consisting of Soccer, Rugger, Hockey, Boxing, Cross Country, Rifle Drill, P.T., .22 Miniature Rifle Shooting, and Commanders' Inspection. The Competition is on a yearly basis, ending in December.

---

## CHAMPION COMPANY
### "C" COMPANY

Commander:

Major J. Hitt, Royal Tank Regiment.

---

The Pipe Band and the Military Band are composed of volunteers from both Apprentice and the Permanent Military Staff of the School.